Knots
Step-by-Step Instructional Guide on Tying Knots For Any Purpose

Disclamer: All photos used in this book, including the cover photo were made available under a Attribution-NonCommercial-ShareAlike 2.0 Generic and sourced from Flickr

Table Content

Introduction 4

Chapter 1 – What is Knot Tying? 7

Chapter 2 – Knot Tying Projects For Sewing 11

Chapter 3 – Bracelet Knot Tying Projects 20

Chapter 4 – Knot Tying Projects For Fishing 45

Chapter 5 – Knot Tying Projects For Kites 60

Chapter 6 – Necklace Knot Tying Projects 64

Conclusion 74

Introduction

In our busy world, we tend to look for ways to have some kind of a hobby to release some of the stress that we are experiencing. Some of us tend to overlook this very important part because we are busy chasing our dreams and aspirations we forgot to do something to release the stress that we have accumulated from the stressful things that we are doing particularly in our respective work.

There are variety of reasons why people tend to skip hobbies such as financial, the avoidance to learn something new, and many more. When it comes to personal experience I am also like that before, I do not have any hobbies because I am lazy to learn something new.

Thankfully, a friend introduced me to this hobby which is called "knot tying" and I never thought that I will get hooked to this kind of hobby because at first, I thought that it was really boring as you are just only sitting tying ropes.

But I was wrong because this hobby is really enjoyable as you can create different patterns of knots that will make you feel satisfied and your experience memorable. Since I learned knot tying all my stress have been reduced especially when I am doing this knot tying after work.

I learned the different techniques to improve my skills in knot tying and diligently done it every day after work which is the primary reason why I mastered it. I am much honored to share my knot tying knowledge to you through this book. This book will be composed of knot tying projects that are very friendly for beginners and you will surely enjoy doing them.

Once you mastered the projects that we will tackle you can level it up by adding some variations on it according to your own preference. At first, it is normal that you will be confused on some areas on a few topics that we are tackling, do not worry, it is normal. Just like me before when I am just starting out there are certain tying positions and methods that I did not got until I practiced it for several times and eventually mastered it.

I suggest that you do not go all the way when doing a certain project, to master the techniques what you need to do is to make it sure that you will get familiarize to a certain step first before you move on to the next step. I tell you it will be tough if you are always doing it all the way because the next time you encounter a different project that has the same steps you will have a hard time doing it.

However, if you will master every step to your heart, the next time you will encounter that kind of tying you will surely not have a hard time thus you can do it effortlessly. An advice that I can give you is you must take an interest in doing this and put the knowledge inside your heart so that you will understand the modules very well.

It does not matter if you have a background about sewing because it does not matter. You will surely learn a lot of things from this book.

Let us not delay your learning, and let us start doing the projects!

Chapter 1 – What is Knot Tying?

Knots are made from the tying or fastening of ropes and cords which is commonly useful and sometimes used for decorative purposes. Knot tying is a practice of bending two rope ends or cord ends by bringing them together and performing different loops that varies on the worker's desire.

The practice of knot tying takes a lot of time, but if you're willing to invest in it, you can be a professional in no time. There are different types of knots that have its own purpose, because first of all not all knots works in the same manner or application. We'll be listing down these kinds of knots:

- **Bend**- *ever wonder what are the knots used for climbing ropes. These knots are what we called bend knots, it is formed by uniting the two ends of the rope or cord of the same line. There are also different types of bend knots:*

- Adjustable Bend- this is the most common one, it is a kind of bend that can be easily adjusted for lengthening or shortening.

- Beer Knot- this is the specific bend applied in constructing slings used in rock climbing as it holds very tight.

- Ashley's Bend- it is a knot used in securing the ends of two ropes together. Like the other common types of knots, it also features two interlocking overhand knots.

- Butterfly Bend- it is the knot used in joining the two ends of two ropes together.

- Albright's Special- it is a bend used for angling, known for its strength, it used to join two different diameters of line.

- Blood knot- this knot is the most useful knot when you're fishing.

- Carrick Bend- this is the bend that is commonly used for very heavy ropes or cords that is too large.

- Harness Bend- it is a bend that can be pulled before securing.

- **Binding-** it is a knot used to keep two objects together.

- **Coil Knot-** these are the knots used to keep ropes and cables together.

- **Decorative Knot-** these are the knots used in decorative purposes, they're commonly made of repetitive patterns of knots or in different shapes.

- **Hitch-** a knot that is tied usually on cables and rings.

- **Lashing-** a type of knot that is used to hold poles.

- **Loop-** used to create a circle in a line.

- **Plait-** sometimes called braid, is made from a single simple line pattern.

- **Slip-** it is the loops contrast, as you pull the loop it can be closed but the slip knot can't be.

- **Slipped-** one great example of a slipped knot is the tying of your shoelace.

- ***Seizing-*** *it is a knot used for holding two lines together.*

- ***Sennit-*** *unlike the plait that has only a simple pattern, this knot has a complex one.*

- ***Splice-*** *takes time to make but the strongest type of knot.*

- ***Stopper-*** *a knot you can see that holds the line inside a hole.*

- ***Whipping-*** *it binds the rope or cord to prevent a line from fraying.*

Although some of these knots are difficult to practice, it is worth knowing that they can be useful in certain scenarios. Sometimes, these knots may save your life, especially when you're lost in the forest or other survival scenarios that you can use these knots.

Chapter 2 – Knot Tying Projects For Sewing

Sewing is also common these days, but people tend to sew automatically nowadays because, for some, manual sewing can take a lot of time and effort. But enough of the automated ones, today we'll tackle about the different knot tying used for sewing, from common ones to the ones you probably didn't hear about.

Starting with the first project. The standard knot in sewing, it is the common way on how to hold the sewing thread into the needle. Some may find it hard doing this especially on the part of inserting the sewing thread into the needle's eye but in reality, the steps are pretty easy. Here they are:

- ✓ Step 1: Hold the sewing thread with your two fingers, it depends on what hand you'll be using, if you're right or left handed, it is not a big deal. These steps will still apply perfectly.

- ✓ Step 2: Bring the sewing thread closer to your two fingers, as having a very long allowance of the thread will make it hard for you to insert it inside the needle. After insert it inside the needle, you might want to wiggle it around so that it will fit perfectly on the hole.

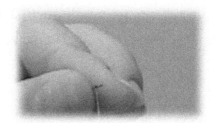

✓ Step 3: When already inserted, pull through until you get in the middle of the sewing thread, when the needle is already there, get the two end lines of the sewing thread and hold them with your forefinger and thumb.

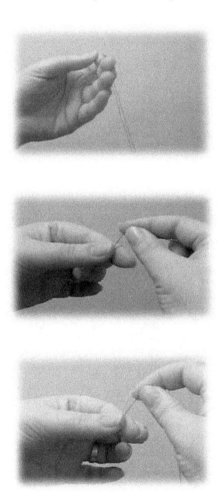

- ✓ Step 4: While holding on the two ends of the sewing thread, start wrapping it up on your forefinger to create a loop. You'll see an 'x', don't put too much allowance on the end line, and just make it short.

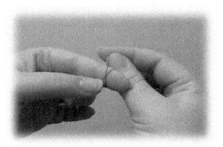

- ✓ Step 5: Hold on to the middle of the 'x' then start rubbing it while pulling slowly away from your forefinger, in this way the end line and the main loop will join temporarily.

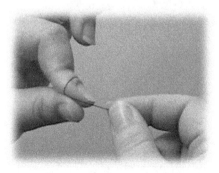

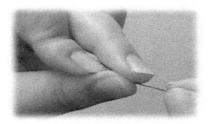

- ✓ Step 6: When the loop reaches the end of your finger, grab the end line of the loop than start pulling it to make the knot.

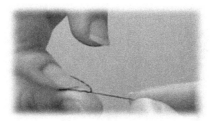

- ✓ Step 7: The knot should like this, and then bring the needle back to that know created after that you're good to go.

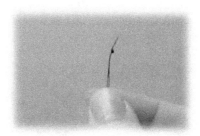

Finishing knot on the back stitch- this step-by-step tutorial will show you on how to properly finish the ending stitch at the back of your fabric or cloth you've been sewing. Pay close attention.

- ✓ Step 1: The front stitch facing you, take the last stitch and push it through the other side using the needle.

- ✓ Step 2: Now flip over the fabric, then you can see the pushed side of the end stitch at the front.

- ✓ Step 3: Insert the needle on that hole created by the pushed end of the stitch at the front.

- ✓ Step 4: When the needle is inserted, stop at the middle. Do not insert it fully.

- ✓ Step 5: You can see two thread endings, one inside the needle and one in the fabric. Grab the one in the fabric.

- ✓ Step 6: After grabbing the end stitch of the fabric, wrap it around the needle three times.

- ✓ Step 7: Then, after making the three wraps around the needle, push it downward and hold it with your thumb and forefinger tightly.

- ✓ Step 8: Then start pulling the needle upwards with your other hand while the other one is holding tightly on the three wraps you made.

- ✓ Step 9: After pulling it upwards, the knot must now appear, then for the final step, cut off the excess thread. Now you have your clean back stitch with a knot.

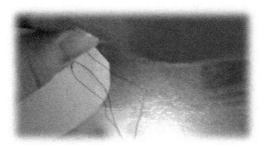

Chapter 3 – Bracelet Knot Tying Projects

Bracelet is a common jewelry and sometimes not all the dazzling jewels or precious stones are the ones that makes it great, sometimes it is the way on how it it's put up. There are some bracelets that are completely made from knots, different knot patterns to be specific.

Having these kind of bracelets will surely make you stand out among others. We're going to show you on how to make a bracelet using these knots.

Simple Adjustable Bracelet- starting off with a standard adjustable bracelet. This is the common knot used in making bracelets, so if you're kinda saving up your time, this step-by-step tutorial is just right for you. It is very easy in you can do this for about five minutes.

Materials needed:

Lighter

Scissors

Two 13" pieces of cord

One 7" piece of cord

A token with a hole of your choice

- ✓ Step 1: Grab one 13" piece of cord, then connect it with both ends.

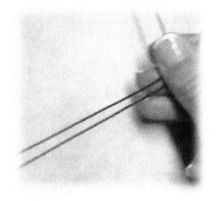

- ✓ Step 2: After connecting it, grab the other end. It should look like this.

- ✓ Step 3: Insert it inside the token but not fully.

- ✓ Step 4: After you inserted the cord, it should look like this.

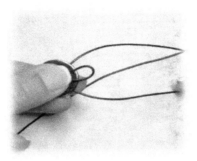

- ✓ Step 5: Grab one part of the cord, then insert it on the loop. Then after that, grab the other piece of cord then insert it on the loop likewise.

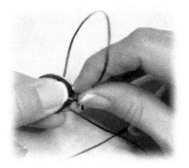

- ✓ Step 6: It should look like this, then after, pull it tightly.

- ✓ Step 7: Repeat step 3 to 6 and you should have this outcome:

- ✓ Step 8: Grab the end points of one cord then tie it. After you tie it, pull it tightly.

- ✓ Step 9: Cut off the excess cord.

- ✓ Step 10: After cutting the excess cord, grab your lighter then melt the end of the cord.

- ✓ Step 11: Repeat step 8 to 11.

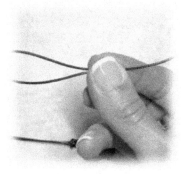

✓ Step 12: Grab the 7" cord then place, put its other end at the middle then place it on the bracelet.

✓ Step 13: Grab the other end of the 7" cord that is sitting at the right hand.

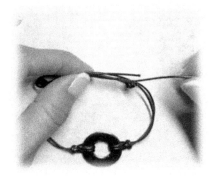

- ✓ Step 14: Wrap it on the bracelet four times. It should look like this

- ✓ Step 15: You will see a loop, insert the excess cord there.

- ✓ Step 16: After you inserted it into the loop, pull it upwards and hold the loop tightly.

- ✓ Step 17: It should like this. Then pull the two lines away from each other. In this way, the cord in the middle will tighten up and lock the bracelet.

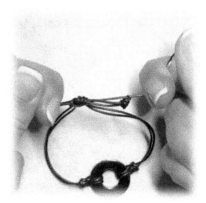

✓ Step 18: Cut off the two excess cords then light up each end to secure the cord.

Now, you'll have a simple adjustable bracelet.

Single Strand Knot and Loop Bracelet- this knot for a bracelet features a locking mechanic, it secures the bracelet and fits it just right for your wrist. It has a simple look into it, so pay attention on how it is done and you might find yourself having a really cool Do It Yourself bracelet!

Materials Needed:

70 cm Cord

Scissor

Lighter

- ✓ Step 1: To start making this really great bracelet, begin by by burning out the cord's two ends.

- ✓ Step 2: Then take about 25 cm on the cord (We're sure that this size is the standard one for bracelets, but it varies depending on the size of your desire.)

- ✓ Step 3: Make a stopper knot, to do this follow the next steps.

Quick Insight about the Stopper Knot: A stopper knot is a not that creates a thick fixed point that serves as a barrier on the other end of the rope to prevent it from sliding off.

- ✓ Step 4: Starting off with the stopper knot. Hold at the part of the 25 cm cord in your left hand tightly (The placement of the hands may vary depending on your dominant hand). And make 2 loops.

- ✓ Step 5: Put a loop on the top of the other loop then grab the cord's end. This will create three loops in total.

- ✓ Step 6: So you can see there are three loops created, insert the cord you're holding on the closest loop. It is the one at the right side of your hand. (Again, the placement of the cord may vary depending on the hands you're using.)

- ✓ Step 7: After you inserted it, next is insert it on the second loop and pull it towards you.

- ✓ Step 8: Then again insert it on the last loop.

- ✓ Step 9: After inserting it on the last loop, pull the cord downward. Don't pull it hard as it will tighten up the knot, we're not yet done here.

- ✓ Step 10: After step 9, insert again the cord to this loop: (Again just insert and pull it slightly, you don't want to lock it down already and be frustrated.)

- ✓ Step 11: After you inserted it. Find the middle loop then insert the cord in then pull it towards you.

- ✓ Step 12: You should have this outcome so far:

✓ Step 13: Adjust and tighten the knot.

✓ Step 14: Cut off the excess cord then light it up to close up the edge.

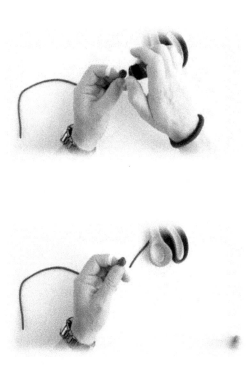

✓ Step 15: Wrap it up around your wrist to measure the size of the bracelet, then fold the cord around the knot. This will let you know if it fits just right on your wrist.

✓ Step 16: Hold the folded cord tightly to prevent it from bursting out.

✓ Step 17: Grab the end of the cord without the knot and wrap it around two times. It will look like the hangman's knot, well defenitely it is a hangman's knot and it will serve as the placement of your stopper knot.

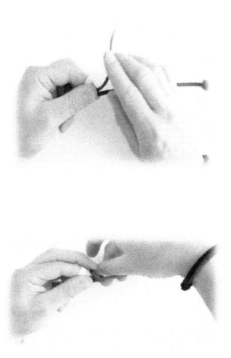

- ✓ Step 18: After making two wrap arounds, insert the cord in it then pull it but don't pull it tight!

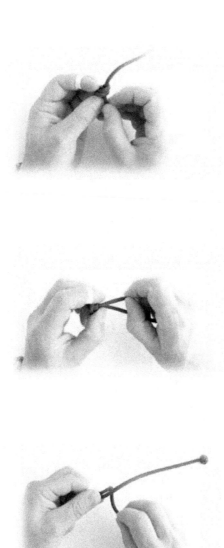

- ✓ Step 19: Tighten the knot slightly so that you'll have an outlook on how it's gonna work on your wrist.

- ✓ Step 20: Wrap around your wrist again and check for the size.

✓ Step 21: Tighten the knot firmly to prevent it from sliding out or bursting out.

✓ Step 22: Cut off the excess cord.

✓ Step 23: Burn the end of the cord. Done.

Chapter 4 – Knot Tying Projects For Fishing

Knot tying is every essential on fishing because it secures the hook with the fishing line by using the proper knot. Fishing line knots may vary from easy to the most complex one, it also takes time to master these kind of knots. So stay tuned, and read carefully on how to make the proper knots for fishing.

Easiest and Simplest Fishing Knot- this knot is the most common and reliable among all other knots used in fishing. Also it is the easiest one to practice and make. All you need is a trusty fishing line and these steps then you're all set.

Materials Needed:

Fishing line

Hook

Scissor

- ✓ Step 1: Prepare the fishing line and hook (The size of the fish line varies on your preference.)

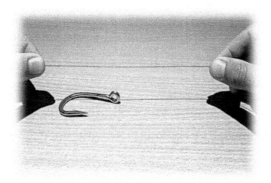

- ✓ Step 2: Insert the fishing line into the hook's eye.

- ✓ Step 3: Grab it until you reach a right length of fishing line. (Again, the length may vary depending on your preference.)

- ✓ Step 4: Start twisting it over and over until there's a small loop created near the hook's eye. (Commonly, eight twists are enough but it still varies on the length.)

- Step 5: When the loop is seen, insert the fishing line.

- Step 6: Then pinch on it

- ✓ Step 7: Start pulling it slowly apart from each other.

- ✓ Step 8: Wet it with water so that it'll be easy for you to pull and tighten it up. The water will make less friction making it easy for you to pull the fishing line.

✓ Step 9: Pull and tighten the fishing line in order to finish the knot.

✓ Step 10: Cut of the excess fishing line

- ✓ Step 10: Cut of the excess fishing line.

- ✓ Step 11: There you have your simple fishing knot.

Improved Clinch Knot- Improve Clinch Knot is a kind of knot that is widely used in fishing. It has a series of twists and ties on the fishing line. Although others may find this knot very complex it is worth the try especially if you want to spice things up in fishing.

Materials Needed:

Fishing Line

Hook

Scissor

- ✓ Step 1: Grab your fishing line (depends on the length of your desire) and hook. Then insert the fishing line into the hook's eye.

✓ Step 2: Pull the inserted fishing line until a certain length. (This length varies based on your own preference.)

✓ Step 3: Pinch the part of the hook's eye together with the inserted fishing line then start wrapping it around the other side of the fishing line for about eight times.

✓ Step 4: There will be a loop created beside the hook's eye, again, pinch and hold it.

✓ Step 5: Insert the fishing line's end you've wrap around on the loop beside the hook's eye.

- ✓ Step 6: Pull it gently.

- ✓ Step 7: Wet it with water, then start pulling it tightly.

Palomar Knot- one of the most common fishing knot, it is renowned as one of the strongest knots used in fishing because of how it is made. Good thing about this is, it's very easy to create. Just follow these steps then you're good to go fishing.

Material Needed:

Fishing Line

Scissor

Hook

- ✓ Step 1: Insert the fishing line in the hook's eye.

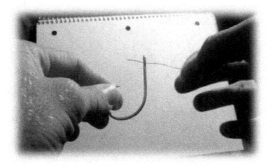

- ✓ Step 2: Pull it continuously until it reaches a right amount of length

- ✓ Step 3: Insert it back on the hook's eye.

- ✓ Step 4: Then slide the hook up the middle of the fishing line.

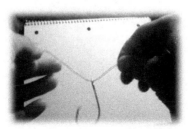

- ✓ Step 5: Insert the fishing line you're holding on your right hand to the loop near your left hand

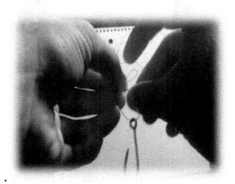

- ✓ Step 6: Then a big loop will form, do not close this loop as you'll be using it on the next step.

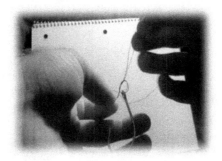

- ✓ Step 7: Insert the big loop over the hook then to the back.

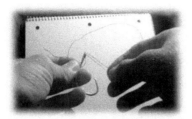

- ✓ Step 8: Pull it tightly to finish the knot.

- ✓ Step 9: You're all set and ready for fishing with the Palomar Knot, one of the strongest knots.

Chapter 5 – Knot Tying Projects For Kites

Some of us brings back the memories of our childhood whenever we see kites around flying in the sky. But today, there is no doubt, even adults are still fond of flying kites. It is not just the kite's design and structure that matters, but also the thing that holds it tight. Different types of knots are used in order to secure kites to their ropes or strings. Here we are going to show you the most common knots used in securing kites.

The Overhand Knot- it is generally used everywhere that needs knot tying, but it is very essential for kite flying as it secures the nylon string or rope you're using that is attached on the kite's body. It may look complicated while making this knot, but honestly it is one of the easiest knots you can make and use perfectly for kite flying.

<u>Material Needed:</u>

String or rope

- ✓ Step 1: Make a loop out of the rope or string.

- ✓ Step 2: Bring the loop in the middle, then insert the remaining rope or string inside the loop.

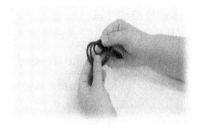

- ✓ Step 3: Then pull it gently.

- ✓ Step 4: Make it tight. There you have an Overhand Knot you can use for flying a kite.

The Larks Head Knot- it is the most commonly used knot for kite flying, it is very easy to make and does not require heavy practice. It secures the nylon string to or rope to the kite's main body so that your kite will fly away.

Materials Needed:

Nylon String or rope used for flying kite

- ✓ Step 1: Insert the loop into the other end of the rope or nylon string.

- ✓ Step 2: Pull it gently.

- ✓ Step 3: Then tighten it up. Remember that this is visual representation of how you could make this knot.

Chapter 6 – Necklace Knot Tying Projects

Necklaces are truly attractive and one of the types of jewelries. And sometimes they can cost us a lot of money whenever we're going to buy them, but what if we tell you that you can make your own fancy necklace just with a few tricks of knots. We're going to list down the different knots used for necklace making.

Adjustable Sliding Knot Necklace- like the adjustable bracelet we've just tackled a while ago. Same steps apply to this knot tying project. It is very easy to achieve especially if practiced perfectly. So if I were you, start practicing making this knot, as you'll surely benefit from this.

Materials Needed:

100 cm cord or string

Scissors

Lighter

Pendant of your choice

- ✓ Step 1: Grab the ends of the string or cord then burn it up.

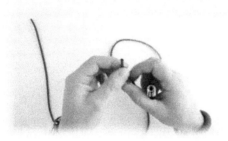

- ✓ Step 2: Fold the cord in half. To do this, connect the cord's both ends together.

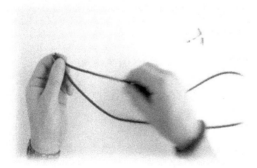

- ✓ Step 3: Insert the pendant on the string or cord and set it aside on the middle of the cord.

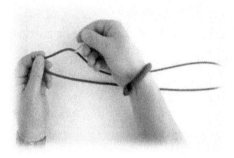

- ✓ Step 4: Take about 20 cm of both ends. (The length of the cord or string may vary depending on the size of the necklace you want to make.)

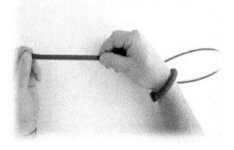

- ✓ Step 5: Cross over the left cord over the right cord.

- ✓ Step 6: Hold it in place and make sure that the loop created will fit in your head.

- ✓ Step 7: Cross around the left string on the right string

- ✓ Step 8: Then start wrapping it up for about three times.

- ✓ Step 9: Then insert the end line on the small loop.

- ✓ Step 10: Tighten the knot slightly.

- ✓ Step 11: Repeat step 7 to 10.

- ✓ Step 12: Check again if it fits in your head.

- ✓ Step 13: Adjust and tighten the knots firmly.

✓ Step 14: Cut off the excess cords.

✓ Step 15: Burn out the edges.

Simple Adjustable Necklace- this knot will show you a simple knot that is commonly used in necklace making. It doesn't take much of your time as you can do this for about 20 seconds because the knot you'll be making doesn't have any complicated steps.

Materials Needed:

String or cord (Depends on your choice)

- ✓ Step 1: Wrap around one string on the other string.

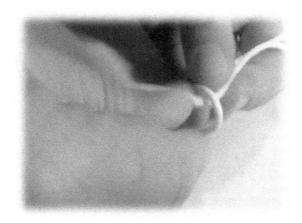

- ✓ Step 2: Repeat it again, now you'll be having two loops.

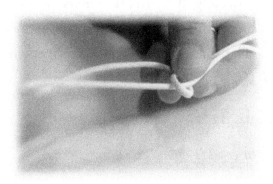

- ✓ Step 3: Insert the other string end inside the loops.

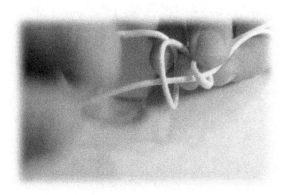

- ✓ Step 4: Then pull it gently, if it locks down, proceed to the last step.

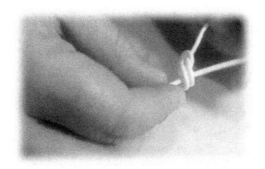

- ✓ Step 5: Tighten it firmly so that the string will not slide over. Then you're all set.

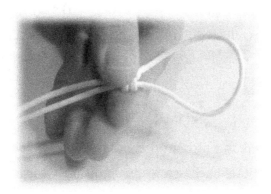

Conclusion

So from all the numerous knot tying projects that we tackled I hope that you learned a lot from it and I am glad that you now have the fundamentals of the different knot tying methods that you can do in the comforts of your own home.

Once you mastered the techniques rest assured that you can do any knot tying projects of your choice in the future. The projects that we tackled are your stepping stone for you to learn and improve.
You can do those projects and other projects that you wish to do with knots on your past time.

Also, if you already think that your works are already excellent you can consider selling them for you to earn some money. Knot tying is in demand nowadays because of their stylish look.

The good thing with knots is that they are considered as multipurpose and you can use it to create different accessories that you can wear to add up some wow factor to your current outfit.

Knot tying is also a great way to help you to surpass crisis situations because they are very useful and can be a way to save lives such as if someone is drowning or there is a need to climb very tall places that do not give you an access to stairs then this is a great way to reach it just like when there is a fire in the area.

No one knows your personally made accessories might be noticed and you can earn a lot of money from it. However, if it does not happen knot tying will teach you a lot of moral lessons such as:

- It will boost your creativity which you can surely apply on your real life as well.

- Your patience will truly be enhanced simply because tying a knot especially if the project is a little bit complicated will require a lot of patience for you not to get bored while doing it.

- It will help you become alert and focus on what you are doing because while tying you must insert the correct knot on a certain opening in order for it not to look awkward and unsafe.

So what I can advice you is to continue practicing for you to perfect this craft as it requires a lot of projects for you to get used to the correct knotting for more desirable results. I wish you good luck and success on all your future endeavors.

www.ingramcontent.com/pod-product-compliance
Lightning Source LLC
LaVergne TN
LVHW022356090125
800953LV00008B/342